Through the
And Other

by

C. R. Hill, Jr.

Patchwork Press, Ltd.
P. O. Box 4684
Canton, Georgia 30115
www.patchworkpress.com

Through the Frosted Window
And Other Christmas Stories

Copyright © 2003
Patchwork Press, Ltd.

Library of Congress Control Number: 2003098284

Scripture taken from the HOLY BIBLE,
King James Version, unless otherwise indicated.

All rights reserved.
Printed in the United States of America.
No part of this publication may be reproduced,
stored in a retrieval system or transmitted in any form
or by any means, electronic, mechanical,
photocopying, recording, or otherwise,
without written permission of the author or publisher.

Published by:
Patchwork Press, Ltd.
P. O. Box 4684
Canton, Georgia 30115
www.patchworkpress.com

ISBN 0-9715925-4-3

Printed in the United States by Morris Publishing
3212 East Highway 30 – Kearney, NE 68847 – 1-800-650-7888

Dedicated to my wife,

Jackie

Table of Contents

Table of Contents

Acknowledgements

This book is dedicated to my wife, Jackie, whose love and support for me, and whose shared involvement in a lifetime of service in the ministry of the United Methodist Church, cannot be praised highly enough. Her faithfulness as a devoted wife, her skill and wisdom as a wonderful mother to our children, and her keen insight and caring touch as a pastor's wife have been a key factor in my being able to fulfill God's call in my life. Far too many times she has graciously allowed her own dreams and plans to take a back seat to the needs of a parishioner or demands of the church. Neither this nor any number of books I write could ever compensate Jackie for the contributions she has made to my life and ministry. Nevertheless, it is my prayer that through this collection of stories, someone will discover the life-transforming grace of God, and Jackie can claim the satisfaction of knowing that she helped make that possible.

I must also acknowledge those congregations who, over the years, have offered inspiration, affirmation, and support of the ministry from which these stories spring: The Winterville United Methodist Church that endorsed my call into ministry when my gifts and graces were yet untested. The early pastorates of Mt. Pleasant United Methodist Church, Redstone United Methodist Church, Temple United Methodist Church, Macedonia/Redwine United Methodist Churches, and Campton United Methodist Church, shaped my ministry and style of preaching. Other United Methodist Churches – Shiloh, Union, Peachtree Road, Conyers, McDonough, and Canton – reshaped my style and enabled my preaching and ministry to grow.

During my years at Peachtree Road and Conyers First United Methodist Churches, it was my privilege to serve on staff with some of the finest men and women God has called into ministry. While serving as Senior Minister of McDonough First and Canton First United Methodist Churches, I have been truly blessed by people who served on my staff. Outstanding among these are Dr. Ross Iddings, Mrs. Gail Matthews, Mrs. Hazel Ray, Mrs. Inez Fears, Rev. Debbie Carlton, Mrs. Ester Brooks, Mrs. Midge Breckenridge, Rev. Eric Morphis, Mrs. Jackie Tarrah, Mrs. Marilyn Lukas, Mrs. Sandy Whitter, Mr. Willie Stalls, Mrs. Robbie Drane, Mrs. Pat Seeks, Rev. Ed Towers, Mr. Steve Klaesius, Mrs. Beverly Dickerson, Mrs. Jennell Bryan, Mr. Collin Stackhouse, Mrs. Nancy Stackhouse, Mrs. Deanie Fincher, Mrs. Cortney Massoud, Dr. Don Stafford, Mr. Glenn Cantrell, Mrs. Janice Cantrell, Mrs. Susan Miller, Mrs. Donna Dobson, and Mrs. Mary Lee Thompson.

There have been others whose contributions are also appreciated.

I must give special acknowledgement to Mrs. Anne Taylor, my secretary at Canton First United Methodist Church. Without her constant assistance with the details of these stories, as well as every aspect of the ministry of the church, this collection would not be possible. Mrs. Monica Taylor, Dr. George Morris, Mrs. Eileen Reynolds, and Mrs. Gail Matthews, were among the first to review the early manuscript and make helpful editorial corrections and suggestions.

Finally, I must say a special thank you to Mrs. Cathy Lee Phillips and Patchwork Press, Ltd. Cathy has served as my Editor and Publisher and has provided priceless advice and counsel, as well as many hours of tedious editing of the original manuscript.

In the end I realize that no meaningful work or act of ministry is the product of one person's efforts. God works through a multitude of individuals, using their collective talents to advance his Kingdom and the goal of transforming people into the likeness of Jesus Christ.

Therefore, if this work has any lasting merit or meaningful significance in your life, then give God the Glory. Amen.

--Dr. C. R. Hill
Canton, Georgia,
September 2003

Preface

Through the Frosted Window is a collection of fictional Christmas stories that began as sermons presented to my congregations.

After years of preaching from the familiar text of Advent, it seemed a good idea to take some of the core truths of the coming of Christ into the world and to present those truths in the form of these stories. It was, and remains, my goal that, through these fictional stories, my congregations could hear with fresh ears the message of God's life-transforming gift to the world; a gift that came in the person of his son, Jesus Christ.

Since first being introduced, these messages have been well-received and long-remember by my parishioners. Congregations have looked forward to having them repeated from time to time. They have also looked forward to having new stories added throughout the years.

The Perfect Gift was the first of these messages. It was first preached to my congregation at McDonough First United Methodist Church in 1995 under the title of *The Crystal Manger*. *The Night of Angels*, first preached under the title of *The Plan* followed it that same year. *The Night of Miracles* and *The Shepherd* followed in subsequent years as Christmas Eve candlelight messages. *Through The Frosted Window* was the 2001 addition to the collection.

It is my custom to write a poem most weeks that lifts some aspect central to the message of my service. I have prefaced each story in this collection with such a poem. Some of these poems were the ones originally written to illustrate the point of the sermon. However, *Joseph's Song* and *Still The Christ Child Fills The Earth* were written especially for this collection and make their first appearance here.

I invite you to enjoy these simple stories and to let your imagination run free. The stories may be fictional, but the messages they contain are profoundly true and can transform your life.

My prayer is that you may experience God's life-transforming love in the gift of his Son as you enjoy these pages.

--Dr. C. R. Hill

The Message of Peace

*The message of peace
that was sung by the angels
on that first Christmas so many centuries ago
still rings today.
It rings in the lives of the millions of people
who receive the Prince of Peace into their hearts
and experience the
"Peace of God that passes all understanding."*

C. R. Hill, Jr.

All Hail The Inward Peace

I've seen the lighted candles
I've heard the joyful song.
'Tis for the peace that angels promise,
That my heart and life do long.

The world around me 's reeling,
My soul with anguish cries
As I consider war and violence,
All the murders, thefts, and lies.

Where is thy splendid kingdom,
O infant Son of Man?
Do you still reign immortal?
Is the world still in your hand?

Ah, in the Book I hear you,
In your presence my troubles cease.
Your love and power reign in me
And your Word fills life with peace.

The Night of Angels

"**M**erry Christmas," smiled the woman sitting next to her as she reached out a lighted candle. Everyone had been given a candle as they entered the church. They were to light their candle then pass the flame to their neighbor to symbolize the Light of Christmas.

"Oh, Merry Christmas," she muttered in return as the congregation stood to sing, "*Joy to the world, the Lord has come.*"

"What am I doing here?" she wondered as she reached inside her coat pocket. Just touching the object concealed there reassured her.

She had deliberately been the last to leave the office at the business of her friend, Millie. She had cut too close rounding the corner beside the church. Her front tire struck a piece of jutting curb and blew out. Almost instantly, the nice young man in the service station jacket and cap appeared beside her car offering to help.

"Pull into this parking lot," he said, "and I'll have that tire changed for you in a matter of minutes."

She pulled into the rapidly-filling church parking lot as the service station attendant instructed.

"Open your trunk and I will get your jack and spare tire," he said.

It was then she remembered the object in her pocket. Until that morning it had been stored under the spare tire in her trunk. To retrieve it, she had removed the spare tire and left it propped against the wall in her carport.

"Ah, ah, I don't have a spare," she muttered.

"Hum," said the young man. "In that case, I have a used tire that will fit perfectly, but it is back at the station. It will take me about an hour to get your tire back there and make the change. You wait in the church where it will be warmer and you will be safe."

He had partially ushered her through the door of the church.

"Joy to the world the Lord has come – let earth receive her King . . ."

The congregation sang the refrain one last time as they held their candles high above their heads. Timidly, she raised her candle and mouthed the words that had so long ago lost all meaning to her.

The minister's hands were raised over the congregation as he pronounced the Benediction by reciting the words of Jesus:

> *"Peace I leave with you,*
> *my peace I give unto you:*
> *not as the world giveth, give I unto you.*
> *Let not your heart be troubled,*
> *neither let it be afraid."*

--John 14:27

The minister concluded, "May the peace of Christmas be with you always. Amen."

The lights came on, the candles were extinguished, and the happy congregation filed out amid a din of laughs and Merry Christmas wishes. In a few minutes, she was standing alone in the sanctuary looking up at the now-empty manger. The minister's benediction still rang in her ears. She shuddered and closed her eyes, trying to blot out the scene and the sound.

"Your car is ready, Ma'am."

Startled, she looked up. The young man in the service station jacket and cap was standing in the doorway.

"Oh! Ah, ah, thank you. How much do I owe you?"

"It was a used tire, Ma'am, but it has some good life left in it. Consider it a Christmas gift. Merry Christmas."

He was out the door and gone before she could thank him again.

The plan she had so carefully detailed on Millie's computer differed in only one respect from her plan for every – or almost every other – Christmas. She left the plan for Millie to find the day after Christmas. She despised Christmas. It was the loneliest, most painful and confusing day of the year for her. She always spent Christmas Eve night driving to some out-of-the-way motel where she holed up and slept through Christmas day. Then she drove all night to get home. She wished to blot out any reminder of the day.

"It is a day of lies," she muttered through clenched teeth as she pulled onto south I-95 heading out of Washington. She punched the accelerator, let the speedometer climb to seventy miles per hour, and locked the cruise control.

"A day of lies! There is no peace. Never was. Never will be!" she uttered bitterly.

The normally crowded corridor of concrete and asphalt was virtually empty as she sped through the Christmas Eve darkness toward Richmond. From Richmond she would drive down the peninsula, past Williamsburg to US 17, then through Norfolk and on to the Outer Banks.

Turning on her windshield wipers to clear away the light mist that started to fall, she fumbled for her taped book of Sheldon's *Windmills of the Gods*. It was filled with just the sort

of international intrigue, murder and power plays that had
characterized so much of her world, real and imagined, for
twenty-five years. Twenty-five years in the Diplomatic Corp.
She had risen to a high-ranking position in the State Department
before her retirement.

"Retirement!"

She spewed the word out loud with anger in her voice.
She knew the retirement was forced because they had lost all
confidence in her ability to keep it together. She had cut her
diplomatic teeth in the Kissinger years of the Nixon
Administration. She had served under six Presidents in all.

"Retirement, indeed."

She knew it was all part of a conspiracy of harassment
that had been mounting against her during the past several years.

"That church service," she thought as she left Interstate 95
and headed down the peninsula, "what a fluke."

She tried to recall the last time she had been in church.
Actually she had been very active in church in her preteen and
adolescent years. But that was what – thirty-five years ago now?

Her mind wondered back to another Christmas Eve. She
recalled another Nativity drama in a little white frame Episcopal
Church in a small Alabama college town. She had been an angel
that year, complete with paper wings and a coat hanger halo. She
had even been the one with the big lines: "Fear not, for behold I
bring you glad tidings . . ."

Her younger sister had been in the angel chorus that sang
"Peace on earth . . ."

She could remember her younger brother as one of the
Wise Men. There he was, a three-year-old dressed in his bathrobe
with a towel wrapped turban-style around his head.

She could not recall what part, if any, her older brother
had played.

"Probably Herod," she said out loud. "He was perfect for
that part."

She stopped for gas at an all-night service plaza on US 17 just north of Norfolk. Even though she planned to end her life before another twenty-four hours passed, she had no desire to run out of gas in the middle of nowhere. She knew just when and where and how she would do it. Every detail was carefully planned, right down to the precise minute the tide was to turn outward.

A short distance further, a Waffle House sign lit up the night sky. She pulled off the highway, parked, and went inside.

"Merry Christmas," called a waitress from the far end of the restaurant. Aside from her, the only other person in the place was the cook. A ruggedly handsome young man in his early to mid-thirties, he had an air of confidence about him that seemed almost out of place in such surroundings.

"Go ahead and make your call, Mary. I'll wait on this lady," he said.

"Just coffee," she requested. "Black, no cream."

Sipping the hot, dark liquid, she contemplated her plan. She would check into the motel then put out the *Do Not Disturb* sign. About thirty minutes before the tide turned out, she would slip out of her room, stroll down the beach road and onto the pier. At the end of the pier she would slither through the railing, lean out as far as she could while holding on with one hand. She would then remove the object from her pocket for one fatal second of service. The outgoing tide would carry her to her resting place.

"Care for a piece of pie?"

"What?" she snapped.

All she had heard was *piece* and she mistakenly thought the waiter had said *peace*, again evoking her anger over the contradiction between the angel's message and the reality of her life. The minister's benediction played again in her mind.

"My peace I leave with you . . ."

Looking up, she saw the cook standing beside her with a generous slice of pecan pie on a plate.

"A piece of pie. It's on the house. After all, it's Christmas."

He sat the plate in front of her and, at the same time, refilled her cup of coffee. As she looked up at him, she noted that his eyes seemed filled with understanding. It was as if he could read her very soul.

"There is no peace," she whispered into her coffee cup. "Not in me, not in the world, not now, not ever!"

"What was that, Ma'am?" the cook asked as he looked up from cleaning the grill.

"Oh, nothing. I was just thinking."

Nervously, she laid a five dollar bill on the counter and turned to walk out.

"Keep the change," she said as she reached the door.

"Thanks," he called after her, "and Merry Christmas."

🎁 🎁 🎁 🎁 🎁

The Outer Banks, a popular vacation spot in the summer months, was a raw, cold place in December. Only a few hardy residents lived there year-round and early on Christmas morning, they would be in the warmth of their homes sharing the holiday with their families.

According to her plan, she checked into the nearly-deserted hotel and started toward the pier. Fog had rolled in, reducing visibility to no more than thirty or forty feet.

"Perfect," she thought as she stepped onto the deserted pier. Walking to the very end, she stood very still, looking into the churning ocean below. She wanted to be certain the tide was running out to sea before she executed the final step of her plan. Standing on the pier, she recounted the events that led her to this moment. Then she recalled the smile of the woman sitting next to her in the church service, the kindness of the service station attendant and the understanding look in the eyes of the cook at the Waffle House.

"Would they have been that nice if they had known the plan?" she wondered.

"I like the ocean this time of year, don't you?"

The words snapped her out of her trance. She had not been aware of anyone else on the pier. She had heard no one walking nearby, yet not ten feet away was a young man dressed in jeans and a navy pea jacket. He was standing erect at the railing looking out to sea.

"Perhaps it is the solitude," he continued. "It is not the same place when all the tourists are here in the summer months. I think it is the ocean itself, though. I find it peaceful. It calms my spirit. When I consider how vast it is and how precisely God set its boundaries and regulates its tides, it reassures me. I imagine that if he can do that with all this water, he can certainly handle the storms that upset the peace in my own life. Don't you agree?"

His head turned toward her as he asked the question.

"Ah, ah, I suppose," she muttered.

She was furious that he had appeared to spoil her plan. She had counted on the pier being empty. This young man showed no sign of being in any hurry to leave. Yet, something deep within her was relieved that he had shown up. Something within her was actually glad, though she still clung to her anger. She turned and walked back to her motel room.

Inside the room she noticed that the Gideon Bible lay open on her nightstand. She picked it up and noticed that it was turned to the Gospel of Luke, chapter two. She read:

"And it came to pass in those days,
that there went out a decree from Caesar Augustus . . .
And suddenly there was with the angel

*a multitude of the heavenly host
praising God, and saying,
Glory to God in the highest,
and on earth peace, good will toward men."*

--Luke 2:1, 13-14

She fell across the bed. The minister's benediction echoed once more in her mind:

*"Peace I leave with you,
my peace I give unto you:
not as the world giveth, give I unto you.
Let not your heart be troubled,
neither let it be afraid."*

She thought again of the white frame Episcopal Church and the Christmas pageant so long ago. She, her sister, and her brother each had a part.

"He was a shepherd," she said as she remembered the older brother. "Herod would have suited him better – at least then."

"I'll give it a week. If things aren't any better by midnight on New Year's Eve, I can do it in my living room and no one will know the difference. Just one more big bang."

She drifted off to sleep, the minister's benediction still resounding in her mind, *"Peace I leave with you; my peace I give to you . . . "*

She sat up suddenly.

"The plan!" she gasped. "It is on Millie's computer. If they find it they will have me committed for sure."

Quickly, she looked at the clock. There was still time. If she pushed it, she could get back before rush hour, go to the office and delete the plan before the others got to work.

It was 7:00 a.m. when she once again left the office complex where Millie's business was housed. The plan was deleted from the computer. As she drove toward her house in the suburbs, she pondered the events of the recent hours. She was the same person. Still divorced for over twenty years. Alone with no children. Retired from the one source of meaning in her life for the last quarter of a century. She was still the daughter of the same parents, the second oldest of four children despite her efforts to distance herself from them. The only difference was that, for the first time in her memory, it was alright. She felt loved, valued, and whole.

An accident stopped traffic ahead of her. She decided to take a detour, one she had sometimes used on her way into town – right through a residential street for several blocks, left on another avenue to the dead-end, another left, and then a right turn. She should bypass the accident and return to the main highway not too far from her street. The streets looked a little strange as she drove the route backwards, but she was on course for the dead-end. She approached the stop sign, stopped, and sat frozen behind the wheel. Before her, just across the street, was a white frame Episcopal Church beautifully bathed in the morning sunlight. And if that were not enough, these now-familiar words filled the message board in front of the church:

"Peace I leave with you,
my peace I give unto you:
not as the world giveth, give I unto you.
Let not your heart be troubled,
neither let it be afraid."

11

Like the sun rising in a cloudless sky she suddenly realized, "These are Jesus' words!"

She whispered to herself, "These are Jesus' words and they are speaking straight to me."

"Yes," she said out loud. "Yes, I believe!"

A moment later, a horn blew behind her. She smiled as she pulled into the intersection and continued on her way. She felt good. For the first time she could remember, she felt really good! As she turned back onto the main highway she also realized that she felt hungry. It had been more than thirty hours since she had eaten anything, and that only a slice of pecan pie.

Just across the interchange with the beltway a Cracker Barrel sign glistened in the morning sun.

"Pancakes!" she thought as she wheeled into the parking lot and brought the car to a halt in front of the rocking-chair porch.

"Pancakes with maple syrup and bacon," she whispered to herself as she entered the store filled with delicious breakfast fragrances.

"Good morning," said a clerk who was arranging leftover Christmas ornaments on a half-price table.

"Good morning," she smiled in reply.

"Good morning and Merry Christmas!"

The Heart of Christmas

*At the heart of the meaning of Christmas
is the reality
that whenever we receive the Christ Child,
who was born upon this night,
into our hearts,
he transforms our lives
by the power of his love.*

C. R. Hill, Jr.

Joseph's Song

My life I thought was going well,
Just the way that I had planned,
Until a stinging blow was dealt,
And I saw my dreams turn into sand.

I fumed within this heart of mine
As I pondered what to do,
For the one I trusted most in life
Had seemed to me to prove untrue.

The pain I felt within my heart
Angels could not drive away.
Even though compelled to carry on,
My anger grew and grew each day.

Then came that night beneath the star
When God cleansed me from within,
As in my arms his infant Son I held,
God transformed my heart through him.

The Night of Miracles

Look at him now. You'd think nothing had ever happened. He is just another twelve-year-old playing with his friends.

Twelve-year-olds, Hrrmph! They are God's way of paying parents back for all the mischief of their own youth. But he does have a wonderful sense of humor, that boy does.

I tell you, I have never in my life had a scare like the one that boy gave his mother and me this week. When we discovered five days ago that he was missing, I panicked. How could I have been so careless? How could I have let him out of my sight for more than a few minutes, let alone an entire day? What if some of Herod's old guard suspected who he was and kidnapped him? How could I stand it if I had let anything happen to him? How could I ever face his mother again? How could I face . . . ?

Silly of me to be so worried.

In the past God has always warned me when he was in danger, and there was no such warning this time. Why, it was as though I, myself, had forgotten who he is and who it is that watches over him. I tell you, when we found him in the temple talking with the elders and speaking to them with such authority and knowledge, I've never known a prouder moment! Oh, how I love and admire that boy.

What a joy and delight he has been to us. What a blessing he is to me.

It amazes me still when I think about it. When I remember those months leading up to his birth, I shudder. How could I have been so blessed and such a fool at the same time? It was more than a sense of humor that led God to select me for this role. It was grace and mercy. It was grace and mercy if ever there was grace and mercy.

Why, I tell you, there never were two people on earth more mismatched than his mother and me. Ours was an arranged marriage from the beginning – arranged because her father owed me a considerable debt he had no hope of ever paying. Not that I objected, mind you; after all, she was young and very beautiful. She was not only beautiful to look at – she was, and remains in every way, beautiful to be around. Never had I witnessed a more pure spirit than the one she possessed. She radiated goodness then. She always has.

I am twelve years her senior, but our contrasts were far more than mere years. I think that was what made it so difficult in the beginning. If she had been more like me, I would not have expected so much. I mean, if she had been the kind of self-serving, vengeful person that I was, I would not have been surprised at all that she became involved with another man just to protest a marriage she detested. But that kind of behavior would have been completely out of character with the person she was and always has been.

Oh, to be sure, I never deserved the likes of her – never in a thousand years. But I had her. She was to be mine! I pulled off the catch of a lifetime when this opportunity fell into my lap – I would accept her as my wife in return for the debt her father owed me.

Why, I was walking on top of the world, but not because I loved her that much. In fact, I really didn't know her. I just knew that she was young and beautiful and a real dream. I had won the hand of the woman who would make me the envy of every man in the village.

16

Then, just before we were to wed, she told me of the child. Suddenly I began to feel as though my dream had become a nightmare. Instead of being the envy of every man in town, I was a laughing-stock. I was furious. I believed that her "angelic personality" was just about the most clever put-on I had ever encountered. I was ready to call the whole thing off, but I had to do it quietly or everyone would know the fool I had been taken for.

I tell you, I was in a dilemma. The law was clear in this case and I have always sought to follow the law. On the other hand if what I believed was actually true, telling the truth about Mary would expose her to very serious consequences. As angry as I was, I did not want to see her suffer harsh punishment. After agonizing over what to do, I decided to divorce her quietly. That was when I had that dream. An angel of the Lord spoke to me through this dream and told me not to fear to take Mary for my wife. Let me tell you, that dream shook me up! Oh, I did what the angel said. I was scared not to, but I didn't like it. I didn't like it one bit.

You would think I could have recognized what a great blessing and honor God was giving me. But not me. No, I couldn't see beyond my own selfishness.

Mary and I were quickly married and, almost at once, I sent her to visit her cousin, Elizabeth. The story we told was that Elizabeth was having difficulty being with child at her advanced age. Mary, we said, was going to help Elizabeth until her child came. That story took care of things as far as the public was concerned.

If anyone suspected anything strange, at least they kept quiet around me. But I was still furious. Oh, how could I have been such a fool? How could I have been so uncaring and insensitive to Mary and what she was going through? Instead of caring for her as I should, I was only thinking about myself and what people were saying behind my back. With her out of sight, anger and jealousy boiled inside me. I felt cheated, used, imposed upon, inconvenienced.

Things continued this way right up until the night he was born.

Mary returned from Elizabeth's home just in time for us to make the journey to Bethlehem to register for Caesar Augustus' taxation. The trip would have been hard on anyone. It was cold and wet. The roads were muddy and travel was miserable at every turn. On top of all this, I had an expectant mother to look after. Oh, how I would give anything to go back and do everything over again. If only I could make it up to her now. If only I could go back and make that ordeal a little easier for her. Why, I don't think I missed a single opportunity to let her know how much trouble she was causing me.

When we finally got to Bethlehem that evening, I pushed and shoved my way through the streets. I stopped at every inn in town but found nothing – not one single room. I returned a second time to the one place where I thought I saw some compassion in the eyes of the innkeeper. He finally consented to let us stay in his stable.

We had barely gotten settled when it became obvious that the time had come for Mary to give birth. We were in a barn, for crying out loud! We were alone and her baby was coming. I called the innkeeper who sent his daughter out to help. The girl wasn't even as old as Mary and had no experience delivering a child. I had helped several times when a cow was giving birth to a calf or one of the sheep was giving birth to a lamb. Well, I don't mind telling you – I was scared!

Just then, the most amazing things started happening. I was there and have thought about it all these years, but I still cannot really explain what happened. It was as though the whole crude stall was transformed. It didn't change, yet it seemed to change. I mean, all at once it did not feel as cold and damp as before. The lamp appeared to burn brighter, too. It was the same ordinary lamp, but it gave off all the light we needed to see clearly. It was all very strange. There was a different smell in the air, too. Not the pungent smell of animals you would expect in such a place, but a sweeter fragrance – like roses in bloom. That's it. Roses. And lots of them, too.

All at once it happened. The baby was being born. And suddenly I knew just what to do. It was as though I had been delivering babies all my life. Mine were the first hands to touch him when he came into this world. I was the one who slapped the breath of life into his little body. I cleaned him up and wrapped him in the clothes the innkeeper's daughter had found for us.

I was the first person to hold him in my arms.

As I stood holding him, before I even handed him to his mother, the most amazing thing of all took place. As I held him in my arms, I suddenly experienced the most powerful love I have ever felt. It seemed to radiate from his little body and, without words, said everything that needed to be said.

My heart melted in that moment. I shed tears of remorse for the feelings I had been harboring and the way I had been acting toward his mother. I saw what a selfish, heartless person I had been. I felt condemned and cleansed at the same instant! Joy welled up within me and a thrill of wonder overcame me. I was transformed then and there. The man I had been died on the spot. I was a new person. I knew it at once as I handed the baby to his mother. I fell on my knees before him and worshipped him. Truly, this baby we named Jesus was, as the angel had said he would be, the very son of God – Emmanuel, God with us.

Amen.

Is this a true story? Is this really the way it happened? Not exactly, because we really do not know.

The Bible does tell us enough to know that Joseph struggled with the decision to divorce Mary. We can surmise that his struggle came from his desire to follow the law because we are told that Joseph was a just man. We also know that he had compassion for Mary and did not want to subject her to the harsh penalties that the law prescribed for one who conceived a child out of wedlock.

We are also told that the angel of the Lord did visit Joseph to tell him not to be afraid to take Mary for his wife. We know that when they should have been spending precious time together as newlyweds, Mary was at the home of her cousin, Elizabeth, in the hill country of Judah. We do know that Jesus was born in a manger because there was no room for them in the inn and that, very likely, they were very much alone when the actual birth took place.

There is one other bit of truth in the story and that is the whole point of my telling it this way.

The truth is this – whenever we receive the Christ Child who was born upon this night, he transforms our lives by the power of his love.

That truth is at the heart of the meaning of Christmas.

The Light of Christmas

God knows each and every one of us.
God knows our deepest thoughts
and reads our hearts like the pages of a book.
That same God has come down to earth
in the person of his Son, Jesus,
to let each one of us know that he knows us.
That same God is with us
to lead us out of
whatever darkness there is in our lives
and into the
light of the eternal life he has planned for us.

C. R. Hill, Jr.

The Searching Shepherd

In search of life I wondering fed,
I had no intent in me to stray.
I nibbled here – I nibbled there,
'Til I was lost by end of day.

Then darkness did around me close.
Wolves let out their hungry moan
While I on a tiny ledge did crouch,
Very scared and all alone.

Then counting all his flock but me,
The Shepherd left the ninety and nine.
Into the dark and dangerous night,
He set out, this sheep to find.

Great dangers did around me close,
My life was racing toward its end,
'Til the searching Shepherd heard my cry,
Then brought me safely home again.

The Shepherd

"He knew me!" he whispered to himself as he lay back on his sheepskin pallet and drew the blanket of wool closer against the night chill.

"How could he know me or anyone? He is a child – an infant only a couple of hours old. Nevertheless, he knew me. When I looked at him sleeping, it was as though he was talking with me about everything that has happened these last two days!'"

Earlier this same night, this shepherd had come to his pallet utterly exhausted. It has been more than thirty-six hours since he had closed his eyes in sleep. The others had taken the early watches, leaving the last watch for him. His faithful sheepdog and companion was curled nearby. Only two years old, the animal had an instinct regarding sheep that belied his youth. It was as though this dog slept with one eye opened for danger.

The sheep, all one hundred of them, were safely in the fold for the night. Relief and joy welled within him as he lay gazing toward the heavens. The heavens were filled with stars so big and bright, it looked as though you could reach up and pluck one like a summer fig from a tree. He thought about his ancestor, David, the shepherd king and recalled the Psalm:

"The Lord is my shepherd;
I shall not want.

*He maketh me lie down
in green pastures:
he leadeth me beside the still waters."*

--Psalm 23:1-2

He breathed a prayer of thanksgiving to God as his mind recalled the events of the last two days.

It had really started the evening before. It had been a rather ordinary day of pasturing his sheep on the hillsides of Judah.

He was a shepherd, just like his cousins who accompanied him. During the day they went their separate ways, each taking their flocks to different areas to pasture them. As darkness fell, though, they all gathered their sheep into a fold together and shared the watches of the night.

His cousins all had larger flocks. But he was proud of his flock that had just reached one hundred sheep that very year. His father, well-known and respected as a shepherd himself, expressed great pride when his son's flock reached one hundred. In fact, his proudest moment had been the day his father entrusted him to take the sheep out to pasture on his own.

The young shepherd cherished each lamb as though it was the family's favorite pet. He easily exhibited a feeling of pride and responsibility that had been instilled in him from an early age.

That pride had turned to horror just the evening before when he counted the sheep passing under his rod as they entered the fold. There were only ninety-nine. Only ninety-nine sheep!

Shep, his dog, had already noticed the loss. The whole time the sheep had been entering the fold, the dog seemed unusually agitated.

Quickly, he called out to the others, "I have a lamb missing. I'm going back for it!"

With only his dog, he started back into the darkness.

"Fool," muttered a hired shepherd who worked for one of his uncles. The others just looked at the man who spoke.

"Well, he is!" the man insisted. "He will never find that lamb now. He is risking his own life for nothing."

"Risking his life, yes," a cousin replied, "but it is not for nothing."

In the darkness, it would have been practically impossible for him to find the pasture where his sheep had been grazing that day. But he had his dog. Shep had the trail at once and was running ahead, barking and leading the way. Still, the shepherd knew that even when they found the pasture, locating one lost lamb would not be easy, even for a skilled dog like Shep. Besides, this was not a good pasture. The grass was scattered in dozens of small clusters. The land was rocky and broken with gullies cutting across it. None of the shepherds relished pasturing their flocks here; however, necessity demanded it when the more suitable pastures were overgrazed.

On this particular day, the flock had been all over the pasture. They had crossed and re-crossed gullies numerous times. They had ventured near very treacherous cliffs. The lingering scent of the flock was everywhere. While the dog knew they were in the right vicinity, it was next to impossible to locate just one small lamb.

They searched the area slowly, inch by inch. With all that was in him, the shepherd wanted to find a living animal. Realistically, though, he knew the chances were against him. At best he probably would find the place where wolves or jackals had devoured the defenseless creature. At the worst, they might never find any sign of the animal at all.

Cautiously, they looked – the shepherd calling and the dog barking in hopes of hearing an answering cry from the lamb.

Then, just as the dawn was breaking, the hoped-for sound was heard. It was Shep's keen sense of hearing that first detected the muffled lowing of a weakened yearling lamb. The shepherd was alerted by the dog's excited barking. Within minutes, the pair had located the frightened animal. The lamb was in a location that had probably saved it from the predators of the night. However, the location presented a new problem – a problem only a shepherd could solve.

The lamb had been grazing near the edge of a deep ravine, a narrow slit in the earth that dropped sharply for almost one hundred feet. The bottom of the ravine was littered with broken and jagged rocks. Evidently, as the animal grazed, the edge gave way under its weight and the lamb fell into the ravine.

But, rather than plunging to its death on the rocks below, the lamb had landed on a small shelf of rock that protruded about ten feet below the top of the ravine. There the tiny creature remained – frightened and unable to move, but safely out of the reach of wolves and jackals.

At first, this location appeared out of reach for the shepherd, too. But, when the lamb fell, the earth had broken away and shifted. There was now a slight indention and a few feet of gently sloping ground in the otherwise straight dropping edge of the ravine. At the head of the slope and about two feet back, grew a small Black Raspberry bush. According to legend, this was the same species that burned without being consumed when Moses receiving his calling from God. This hardy little bush had a root system that went everywhere in search of water. That Black Raspberry bush was the shepherd's one hope.

Around his waist was a small but sturdy rope that the shepherd wore like a girdle coiled more than a dozen times. Into that girdle he had tucked his sheathed shepherds' knife – the same knife his grandfather had carried when he had tended flocks in these hills. The rope was used mostly to draw water, for many of the wells were deep and water was far from reach. As slender as it was, the shepherd had tested the rope's strength before and knew that it would support his weight.

He fastened one end of the rope to the bush, hoping all the while that the root system of the bush was at least as strong as the rope. Next, he crawled to the edge of the cliff and slowly descended. The rope was just long enough to allow him to lower himself onto the shelf – it did not reach all the way. Nor did he dare trust the bush to support all of his weight as he climbed back up.

Taking the shepherd's knife he had held in his teeth during his descent, he began to hollow steps out of the rocky soil. These were no more than small holes into which he could slip his feet, but they would help support his weight as he made his ascent to the top. When he had hollowed out as many steps as possible while standing on the shelf, he slipped his foot into the first hole. Then, taking hold of the rope, he began working his way back toward the top . . . one step at a time. He again carried the knife in his teeth, stopping as necessary to hollow out another step with one hand while holding the rope with the other. He worked for more than an hour.

When his task was complete, he again lowered himself to the shelf of the rock where the lamb lay curled in confused confidence as the shepherd worked. Then, stripping himself almost naked, the shepherd took his outer garment and made a sling into which he bundled the lamb. He then tied the corners securely into a knot. With his inner garment, he extended the length of the rope, tying one end to the rope and the other to the bundle containing the lamb. Then, with his nearly-naked body shivering against the cold of the early winter morning, he carefully climbed to the top of the ravine. All the while, his faithful companion watched with admiration as his master worked deliberately at the rescue.

Slowly, carefully, the shepherd raised the bundle containing the lamb. He took pains not to let the bundle slam into the side of the cliff, knowing this could injure the lamb or cause the bundle to come untied. At last, it was safe. The shepherd untied the bundle and redressed. Meanwhile, Shep excitedly scolded the lamb and attempted to herd it further from the edge of the cliff. The animal took a few wobbly steps and then collapsed from exhaustion. Putting the lamb on his shoulders, the shepherd and dog made their way back to the sheepfold.

By the time they arrived where the others were, it was already past time to take the flock out to feed. All day long, whenever the flock moved, the shepherd carried the weakened lamb. He would put it down to feed, then pick it up and move it to another location. By evening, the lamb was strong enough to walk on its own again. All the way to the sheepfold, the lamb did not leave the side of the shepherd.

The shepherd had been laying on his pallet, gazing up at the stars and recounting the events of the previous night when,

"lo, the angel of the Lord came upon them,
and the glory of the Lord shone round about them:
and they were sore afraid.
And the angel said unto them,
Fear not:
for, behold, I bring you good tidings of great joy,
which shall be to all people.
For unto you is born this day in the city of David
a Saviour,
which is Christ the Lord.
And this shall be a sign unto you;
Ye shall find the babe
wrapped in swaddling clothes,
lying in a manger.
And suddenly there was with the angel

a multitude of the heavenly host praising God,
and saying,
Glory to God in the highest,
and on earth peace, good will toward men.
And it came to pass,
as the angels were gone away from them into heaven,
the shepherds said one to another,
Let us now go even unto Bethlehem,
and see this thing which is come to pass,
which the Lord hath made known unto us.
And they came with haste,
and found Mary, and Joseph,
and the babe lying in a manger.
And when they had seen it,
they made known abroad
the saying which was told them concerning this child.
And all they that heard it
wondered at those things which were told them
by the shepherds.
But Mary kept all these things,
and pondered them in her heart.
And the shepherds returned,
glorifying and praising God
for all the things that they had heard and seen,
as it was told unto them. "

--Luke 2:9-20

"He knew me!" He spoke the words out loud to the night.
"He knew me, I know he did! It was as though he was talking to me about all that happened with the lamb, and he told me he had come to seek and save his lost lambs, just as I had mine."

Now, did this happen just like the story suggests?

It could have, but probably not.

Was the shepherd in Jesus' parable of the lost sheep really one of the shepherds who came to the manger on the night of his birth? We really do not know.

But some things we do know and hold to be true. We know that there were shepherds keeping watch over their sheep that night. We know that the angel of the Lord appeared to them with the wonderful news.

We know that God knows every person on earth and every story of how they have come to where they are. We know that God knows each and every one of you. We know that God knows your deepest thoughts and reads your heart like the pages of a book. We know that God has come down to earth in the person of his Son, Jesus, to let you know that he knows you. And we know that God is with you always – to lead you out of whatever darkness there is in your life to the light of the eternal life he has planned for you.

The Gift of Transformation

*To a world torn by
violence, terrorism, injustice, and war,
God has given the gift of his Son,
whose presence in human lives
transforms hearts,
brings hope,
and leads people in the way of peace.*

C. R. Hill, Jr.

An Echo In The Mountains

What will end this day of madness
In which terror rules the earth,
Where children do in danger stand,
From the very day of birth?

Is there no end to hatred's ways
That death and mayhem spread?
Will Satan rule the hearts of men,
'Til all the earth is dead?

Take heart, O children born of hope,
Let not these evils you dismay,
For God on high has sent his Son
And his Kingdom is on its way.

So shout the news to every land,
Let earth's mountains their echoes ring,
That every knee on earth will bow
And every tongue say Christ is King.

The Christmas Cookie

Another icy blast of wind whipped up sand and sent it driving into his face. He cursed as he started wiping his eyes with the back of his hand.

"I ought to be used to this by now," he muttered halfway out loud.

Actually, he was less angry at the wind and sand now than he had been on other occasions. The sand in his eyes had tugged at the tears lurking just beneath the surface. Though he would not admit it even to himself, it was a momentary release of what he had been feeling ever since watching the little procession of people make their way out of the village earlier that morning.

He was exactly where he wanted to be. He was doing exactly what he had vowed he would do that September morning when rage and vengeance seized his heart. He had grown up hard on the streets of Brooklyn. After two years of community college he had enlisted in the army.

On the morning of September 11, 2001, he was a three-year veteran Staff Sergeant with the U. S. Army Special Forces. He was home on reenlistment leave on that infamous day in September. He had vowed that he would hunt down and kill every person he could find who was even remotely responsible for these cowardly attacks.

Nothing had ever pleased him more than to have been among the initial forces that invaded Afghanistan in search of

Osama bin Laden, his al-Qaida network, and his supporters. They had stormed the strongholds and hideouts, dealing death and destruction without remorse. This was justice.

He was still a part of the occupying forces that remained in Afghanistan as they awaited redeployment in Iraq, or wherever this War on Terror took him next. He had watched as that little procession of people rekindled and fanned the fires of feelings raging within him − feelings of sorrow and anger, love and hate, and a longing to set things right that could never be set right in a million years.

Two days before he was sharing Christmas cookies from a tin his sister had sent. The little fellow was about the same age as his four-year-old nephew, though smaller by several inches and a good fifteen pounds. It was that same nephew who had saved his sister's life with his suffering on that fateful September morning.

Late in the evening of September 10, his nephew developed a fever. His parents paid little attention to it at first. They gave him the usual Tylenol and tucked him into bed. Around 2:30 a.m. they were awakened by the child's cry. When they checked him, they realized his fever had spiked to 104 degrees. His parents called their physician and were instructed to meet him at the Emergency Room of their local New Jersey hospital.

It was 7:50 a.m. when both mother and child arrived back home. Her husband, a firefighter at a New York suburban station, took a cab from the hospital and went straight to work where he always kept a spare uniform. There was nothing the mother could do but call the office and advise her boss that she would be late for work. Forty-five minutes later, her mother-in-law arrived to stay with the child. The mother was on the way out of the door a few seconds before nine when she heard Charlie Gibson's voice from the TV in the other room. His words arrested her in her tracks. Rushing into the den, she saw smoke billowing from the building that housed her office. She worked on the seventy-second floor.

🎁 🎁 🎁 🎁 🎁

This little guy had become his buddy a few months earlier, after the initial fighting had subsided. At first he would come around only at meal times. He stood at a distance watching him eat, just like a puppy waiting for a scrap. After a few days, he motioned the little fellow over and divided his meal with him. He wrote his sister about the child and she responded by sending a package containing a pair of shoes, some socks, a stocking cap and sweater. She also mailed other items including coloring sheets and crayons. The Christmas cookies she sent were intended for her brother. Of course, she knew he would be sharing them with his little friend.

Oblivious to the symbolism of the shape of the cookies, the little fellow gobbled down the first one offered. Then he held out his hand for another and another.

Why was he drawn to this child? He knew that it was more than the fact that the little guy reminded him of his nephew. Despite the fact the child was from a Muslim family, he could not refuse those brown eyes and the starving frame of a boy. He gave him first a Santa, then a Christmas tree, then a star, and then an angel. In fact, he ate only a couple of the cookies himself. When they got to the last cookie in the tin, he held it out with one hand. His little friend took hold of the cookie as well and they broke it into two unequal parts. Of course, he made sure that the little fellow got the larger portion, which he ate at once. He took the remaining part and slipped it into his jacket pocket. As always, the child repaid this generosity with a warm smile and big hug. Then, content and happy for the moment, he ran off to play with the other children.

Again he muttered an oath as he fought back the tears that came this time unaided by a blast of wind-driven sand. Anger burned within him as he thought of that little procession of people walking mournfully from the village and making their way to the cemetery. Again he wanted to take revenge on those responsible, but who would he target this time? The Russians? The Afghan rebels? The Taliban? Or himself and his men for missing this one on their sweep of the area?

It had been only an hour or so after sharing his cookies with him that the little chap had stepped on an old Russian land mine while playing with other children. Most of the mines had been cleared from the area. However, there were still some mines that had been covered by exploding shells and were brought closer to the surface once more by eroding winds or other forces. Usually these mines left a child without a foot or a leg. In this case, though, the child was too small, too frail, and the bleeding was too profuse. The little guy had bled to death before the first adult could reach him.

🎁 🎁 🎁 🎁 🎁

It was night. Nearly a month had passed since that little procession of people made their way out of that Afghan village on their mission of sorrow. He checked his watch. 23:15 and forty-five seconds.

Suddenly a gust of wind whipped the sands of another desert into his face and he remembered. But something was different about him now. Somehow, just knowing that little fellow had changed him. To be sure, he still had no illusions about the nature and intent of the enemies he and his men were battling.

36

He knew them to be people driven by a hatred that was beyond reason. They would stop at nothing, spare no innocent life, and make whatever sacrifice necessary to advance their mission of murder and destruction.

It had barely been a month since the little boy had died. But in that time he had witnessed far too many similar processions for the same mournful purpose. These gatherings bore witness to the harsh realities of relentless terrorism. And these gatherings made him more resolute than ever to use whatever force required to contain these people.

The wind gusted again and he brushed the sand from his eyes. But there were no tears this time – only the realization that his reasons for wanting to fight this war were changing. No longer was he driven by anger and the passion for revenge. Hate and malice towards these people no longer dominated his feelings.

"Where did that go?" he wondered to himself.

The events he experienced since his arrival in Afghanistan had opened his eyes to the futility of revenge. He began to see the war almost as one huge family feud filled with murderous perpetrators, accidental victims, and unrightable wrongs. Tragically, all parties were trapped in a never-ending, always-escalating cycle of retaliation.

And what about the disappearance of the hate he once felt toward all people responsible for that horrible September morning? Well, there was no mystery there! His hatred was melted by the simple love of a four-year-old. It was clear that he was there to do everything possible to prevent future processions of mourners. In fact, if he could prevent just one more procession, it would be worth everything. He was convinced that by making it harder for al-Qaida operatives to have a base of operations, he and others were helping to contain terrorism. Yet despite their determination to use whatever force available to hold these terrorists in check, he could not help but wonder out

37

loud, "Is there really any power that can bring this madness to an end?"

He shielded his face against another blast of wind-driven sand, then checked his watch. The digital display read 24:2502. He stated it aloud.

"Twenty-four twenty-five o two. Twelve twenty-five o two. It's Christmas Day!"

Reaching into the breast pocket of his field jacket with his ungloved hand, he searched for the letter he had recently received from his sister. He just wanted to touch it again. But, he found something else instead, and it arrested his thoughts. Pulling it out, he held it high against the night sky. It was the wing and head of a Christmas cookie angel. It was his portion of the last cookie he shared with the little Afghan boy. Again, he remembered the child. He remembered how the child's love – in a place so deprived of love – had affected his life. So different they were, yet they were bound together in the sharing of a Christmas cookie. Or was it the cookie that had bound them?

Suddenly, he was looking beyond the fragment of the cookie to the star-filled night sky. One star seemed to be shining brighter than all the others.

Staring at the broken cookie while the bright star shone above it in the night sky, words from his own boyhood floated into his mind:

"And the angel said unto them,
Fear not:
for, behold, I bring you good tidings of great joy,
which shall be to all people.
For unto you is born this day in the city of David
a Saviour,
which is Christ the Lord.
And this shall be a sign unto you:
Ye shall find the babe

wrapped in swaddling clothes,
lying in a manger.
And suddenly there was with the angel
a multitude of the heavenly host praising God
and saying,
Glory to God in the highest,
and on earth peace, good will toward men."

--Luke 2:10-14

"Yes!" he said out loud. "There is a power that will bring this madness to an end."

C. R. Hill, Jr.

The Perfect Gift

There is one central and essential element of truth
in Christmas
that overrides all of the myths,
sacred or secular,
which surround its observance.
That truth is that in Jesus Christ,
God has come among us
and given each of us who receive him a gift –
the power to become his children.

C. R. Hill, Jr.

Infant Child

An infant child in a crib of hay,
Two thousand years ago.
What has his birth with me to do,
As through my life I go?

An infant child from God to man,
Who later died upon a tree.
Is there aught in his life and death,
That effects what I turn out to be?

Ah, infant child of Mary's womb,
Whose breath the world began,
Have you now come in human form
To redeem the sons of man?

Oh, infant child whom angels greet
While skeptics blink and nod,
Come and dwell within my heart,
That I might become the child of God.

The Perfect Gift

For The Person With Everything And Nothing At All

Macy's was closing as he walked out of the store and down the corridor of the mall where the ATM was located. He was a millionaire several times over, but he seldom carried more than fifty or sixty dollars at a time. This Christmas Eve he hardly had cab fare as he purchased a few remaining gifts to take to Roger and Betty's house for Christmas with their family and a few friends.

"How quickly the mall empties on Christmas Eve," he thought to himself as he walked to the ATM and began his transaction.

Macy's had been almost deserted when he had arrived at 4:45 p.m. It was now a few minutes after six. His transaction completed, he turned to start back down the mall toward the entrance where the cabs parked. Just then his eyes fell on the window of a strange little shop directly across from the ATM. The name of the shop was printed on the window in large gold letters outlined in hunter green – *THE PERFECT GIFT*. Then, in smaller letters underneath were the words: *FOR THE PERSON WITH EVERYTHING AND NOTHING AT ALL.*

"This I have got to see," he thought as he started through the door of the shop that was still open.

"Good evening," came the greeting from a small-framed man of obvious oriental ancestry with an accent to match. "What I can help you with tonight, sir?"

43

"I was interested in your sign," said the millionaire. "A very interesting name for a shop."

"Ah," said the little man. "We have many very special gifts in shop. You look around. You find something, okay?"

The millionaire glanced around the shop. It was indeed filled with a marvelous assortment of unusual and expensive-looking gift items. However, nothing struck him as "the perfect gift for the man who had everything."

"You do indeed have a wide variety of things to choose from," he said to the shopkeeper at last. "But your sign led me to think there was even something better here than I see."

"Ah," said the shopkeeper. "You gentleman who is interested in most special gift of all. You wait here. I bring out most special gift."

From a little room in the back of the store, the shopkeeper called out, "You are interested in most special gift for yourself, yes?"

"Why, yes . . . yes, as a matter of fact, I am. How did you know?" asked the gentleman.

Reappearing from the back with a small exquisitely-wrapped box about five inches cubed, the little shopkeeper said, "Most special gift of all already given. Can only be received now."

Looking at the beautiful box, the millionaire asked, "What is it? Let me see."

"Cannot open until Christmas morning," replied the shopkeeper.

His curiosity was pricked. He had to have this little box, if for no other reason than to know what it contained.

"How much!" he demanded.

"Price on inside," replied the shopkeeper. "You like, you keep, you pay price. You not like, you bring back, no pay price."

The millionaire was ecstatic. One could not get a better deal than that.

"Agreed!" he said. "Shall I sign a ticket?"

"Not necessary," replied the shopkeeper. "I know who you are."

"Thank you," he said as he exited the shop with the mysterious package in his hand.

"Not open until Christmas!" the shopkeeper called after him.

As he dined alone in an almost-deserted little uptown restaurant, he could not stop staring at the beautifully-wrapped box.

"What is it?" he wondered.

He made his way back to his penthouse apartment where he lived alone. He placed the tiny box under the tree along with the other gifts he had received from family, friends, and associates. Its size paled beside the other elaborately-wrapped boxes. But the box's exquisite wrapping captured every ray of light that danced across its surface, suggesting that it did indeed contain a priceless, wonderful treasure. Not since he was a boy could he remember being so excited about a package under the tree. He could hardly contain his curiosity. Still, he enjoyed the anticipation so much that he did not want to rush it.

"I will wait until morning to open it," he promised himself as he spoke out loud.

That night he hardly slept for wondering what might be in the box. However, when morning came, he decided to wait and open the box last, so that he could savor his excitement as long as possible.

He was a person who demanded perfection in his possessions. Yet, his appetite for things was quite modest for a man of his means. His other gifts were all items suited for his taste and stature. They ranged from a full set of the latest and finest golf clubs to a diamond-studded pen and pencil set.

The other gifts opened, the time had finally come to open the mysterious little box containing what the shopkeeper had described as "the most special gift of all." Nervously, he unwrapped the beautiful paper. He was so excited that he did not even care about what the price might be.

Inside the box was white tissue paper protecting the contents. Carefully he removed the loose paper and removed a small object from the center of the box. He gently removed the final layer of white tissue paper protecting the extraordinary object. As the paper fell away, he beheld a beautiful crystal and gold manger with the figure of a baby asleep on the hay of gold. Letters of gold on the side of the manger proclaimed the message:

"But as many as received him,
to them gave he power
to become
the sons of God . . ."

--John 1:12

Sitting very still, the man held the small manger in his hand for a long while. It was beautiful. Indeed, he could not recall seeing a manger more lovely anywhere, and he had seen hundreds – no, thousands – of mangers in nativity scenes.

"What really makes this 'the most special gift of all,'" he wondered. He placed the tiny manger gently on the table and began to examine his other gifts again. He took some practice putts on the living room rug with the new "can't miss" putter that had been a gift from his brother. Then, he dressed for an early-afternoon dinner and Christmas gathering at the home of one of his closest friends.

As he was about to walk out of the apartment, he picked up the tiny manger one more time. The workmanship in the miniature Christ Child was superb. The manger itself was fine crystal. The hay was crystal plated in gold and, for all the world, looked just like real hay. The Christ Child was crystal with the gold of the hay refracting through him in such a way as to give him an olive-gold flesh appearance. The detail in the face of the sleeping child was so lifelike that he found himself holding his breath to keep from waking him. Still, he could not help but admit his disappointment as he gently placed the manger back on the table.

"It is beautiful," he thought, "but I've seen thousands of mangers with the Christ Child. So, what is really so special about this one?"

He walked to the street, hailed a cab, and was quickly on his way to his afternoon engagement. Only occasionally that afternoon did he think about the manger. Instead, he enjoyed the good company and fine surroundings of his friend's home. Betty, Roger's wife, had a good eye for beauty and excellent taste in decorating. Their home, all dressed up for the holidays, was one of the most beautiful he had ever seen. It was always lovely, but especially so at Christmas. In the library, he paused to admire an olive wood nativity scene Betty had displayed on a table. He made a mental comparison of the workmanship in this hand-carved olive wood manger with that of his own crystal manger and Christ Child. There was no comparison. His was superior by far. Still, it was just a crystal manger with the Christ Child.

Later, as he overhead two of the children talking about the true meaning of Christmas and the birth of a Savior, he tried to recall the inscription on his crystal manger.

"Something about children," he thought. "I'll have to check it out again when I get home."

The day passed quietly and uneventfully. Everyone present brought gifts to exchange. There were joyful laughs and thank-yous as, one by one, the gifts were opened. Then, there was coffee in the library for the adults while the children enjoyed cookies and hot chocolate in the playroom. By 7:45 p.m. he was in a cab on his way to his downtown penthouse apartment.

The phone was ringing as he opened the door to his apartment. He rushed to answer it. His sister, half a continent away, was calling to say "Merry Christmas." She asked about his day. They chatted about the holiday and some of their more elaborate gifts before saying good night.

He started to tell her about the crystal manger, but stopped.

"She would probably ask what was so special about it. And she would probably say that there was nothing unique about a manger at Christmas," he thought to himself.

He retired early that evening. The next day would be a busy workday in the fast-paced world of finance so he needed a good night's sleep. But sleep eluded him. His thoughts returned again and again to the crystal manger.

"What was that inscription?" he wondered. "I meant to check that when I came home."

Getting up, he went into the living room. He turned on the lamp by the table and examined the manger more closely.

> *"But as many as received him,*
> *to them gave he power*
> *to become*
> *the sons of God . . ."*

He read the words aloud.

"I have heard this somewhere," he thought. "I am sure it comes from the Bible someplace."

He replaced the manger on the table, turned out the light, and went to bed. As he drifted off to sleep, the words on the manger kept running through his mind:

> *"But as many as received him,*
> *to them gave he power*
> *to become*
> *the sons of God . . ."*

🎁 🎁 🎁 🎁 🎁

He was asleep and dreaming. Strange dreams floated in and out of his consciousness. In one dream he was on a crowded dirt street in an ancient eastern village. A crowd had gathered around a little stable where some shepherds were chattering frantically – saying something about angels.

Then he was on a green hillside beside a beautiful sea. A large crowd was there and a tall, handsome man with a beard was talking to them about a Kingdom that was coming. Once, he was standing in a crowd on a narrow cobblestone street in an ancient city. Criminals on their way to be executed were being paraded through the street by soldiers. One man had been severely beaten and abused. He resembled the man who had been talking to the crowd by the sea.

Another time, he was in a cemetery. There was a woman weeping frantically while a gardener talked and tried to comfort her. He was too far away to hear their conversation, but he noticed the woman suddenly drop to her knees in amazement – as though she were worshipping the gardener.

The dreams left and he drifted into a deeper sleep. Then, he dreamed again. It was as though he were floating upward through blue skies over green valleys and towering mountains. He then stood on a beautiful plateau. Suddenly, a figure appeared a short distance away – a beautifully brilliant figure in a flowing robe of white, though transparent as crystal. His face shown like the sun and his hair was gold. In a moment, this figure was joined by other figures also clothed in flowing white robes transparent as crystal. Their faces shone like the sun and all had hair of pure gold.

"It is Christ!" he gasped, "but who are those with him?"

The words of the inscription returned to him:

"But as many as received him,
to them gave he power
to become
the sons of God . . ."

He awoke and sat straight up in the bed. The morning sun was shining full-strength into his room.

"That's it!" he shouted out loud.

"That's it. That is what made this the most special gift of all. It is the power to become the children of God."

He dashed into the living room and picked up the crystal manger. The shopkeepers words rang in his ears, "The price is in the box. You like, you pay the price. You no like, you return. I know who you are."

Eagerly, he searched the box and the wrappings. There was no price tag! But, of course, he would keep the manger.

He dressed quickly and rushed out of his apartment to hail a cab.

"To the mall," he told the driver, "the one near the exchange." Moments later he was rushing inside.

"I must tell the shopkeeper that I lost the price tag but I will pay him for the manger. Truly, it is the most special gift."

He dashed past the large department store where he had been shopping the night before last. He turned down the corridor across from the ATM where he had gotten money for cab fare. He finally spotted the sign in the window of the strange little shop. Suddenly, he stopped dead in his tracks. Right where the shop had stood there was actually no shop at all – only a large, half-empty room with scattered fixtures, tables for a restaurant, paint cloths and ladders. And it was obvious that the work had not just begun. In fact, a painter worked diligently in the far corner of the room.

"Hey!" cried the millionaire. "Where is the shop that was here the night before last?"

"What shop?" replied the painter. "This is a restaurant we have been remodeling for a month. There has not been any shop here."

"No! A shop was here. I was right here on Christmas Eve. I bought a most wonderful gift here. Look, it was right in front of the ATM. I know this is the place!"

Confused, the man searched the mall over, retracing his steps from two nights before. The shop existed no place else in the mall. Each time, he returned to the same place in front of the vacant restaurant.

"I know it was here!" he muttered to himself as he turned to leave.

Just then, his eyes fell on a brightly-colored scrap of wrapping paper wadded up by the entrance to the vacant restaurant. He picked it up. It resembled the paper in which the box containing the crystal manger had been wrapped.

Carefully, he unfolded it, and then he stood still with his mouth opened and tears running down his face as he read the words scribbled on the back of the paper . . . *"For you, most special gift of all."*

C. R. Hill, Jr.

Through The Frosted Window

Faith is like looking through
a frosted store window at Christmas time.
You cannot quite see it,
but you know there is something wonderful
beyond the glass.
Miracles are the glimpses of reality
that are beyond the frosted window --
God's reality that is yet to come.

C. R. Hill, Jr.

Still The Christ Child Fills The Earth

Where is the Christ the shepherds saw,
The one whose birth the angels sang?
Where is the man whose mighty works
From choirs and church bells rang?

Where is the one the Prophets said
Would fill the world with peace?
Where is the Jesus who heals the sick,
And does the soul from sin release?

Ah, he is here for the eyes of faith
To discern moving through the earth.
The blind still see, the lame still stand,
And the human soul finds its worth.

Still when the human soul will reach
In faith beyond the veil of earth and time,
It can take hold the very hand of Christ,
And the heights immortal climb.

Through The Frosted Window

"**A**nything I can do for you before I leave?" Jim asked as he rose from the chair beside Bob's hospital bed.

"No," Bob replied with a peace in his voice that had not been there on Jim's previous visits.

"I am okay with it now. I have peeked through the frosted window."

Jim smiled as he took Bob's hand and led them in a short prayer.

Back in his study alone, Jim was still smiling. Rarely does one witness such a complete transformation of attitude and readiness as he had seen in this parishioner and friend who was battling a serious form of cancer.

"It all happened so quickly," he thought.

Two days before Bob had still been the bitter agnostic that Jim had known him to be for most of his adult life. The cancer diagnosis months earlier had only served to aggravate Bob's attitude of doubt and anger toward God.

"Two days ago a bitter and angry man," Jim mused to himself, "and today a peace with God that was a miracle to witness."

Everything seemed to turn around when Jim had said something on his visit two days before. In another angry outburst, Bob raged about the impossibility of knowing anything about God in this life.

Jim responded, "Faith is like looking through a frosted store window at Christmas. Though you cannot quite see it, you know there is something wonderful beyond the glass. Miracles are the glimpses of the reality that are beyond the frosted window – God's reality that is yet to come."

"Now where in the world did that come from?" Jim wondered as he leaned back in his chair and closed his eyes in thought.

🎁 🎁 🎁 🎁 🎁

"You alright, son?"

Someone called from the curb as the seven-year-old picked himself up from the sidewalk and fought back the tears of pain from his banged head and wounded pride.

"Yes, I think so," he muttered.

The homemade cart he had been standing on had suddenly rolled, spilling him onto the damp concrete of the sidewalk. Jimmy was short, even for a boy of seven, and he had been standing on the cart to peer at the display of red scooters, red and white tricycles, and other items arranged in the frosted window of Mr. Wilburn's Western Auto Store on Main Street.

Even standing on his tiptoes in his cart, he could barely see the bicycles. They were leaning on their kickstands in a neat row near the back of the store. It was still there! A bright red and white twenty-six-inch bicycle with chrome rims and handle bars. It had a light on the front fender that took two flashlight batteries and a luggage rack on the back that was perfect for carrying a passenger.

"Still there, but it might as well be a million miles from here as far as I am concerned," he pouted to himself as he started down Main Street pulling his wobble-wheeled cart.

The cart was a homemade combination of old orange crates, a three-foot piece of 2 x 8, two pieces of 2 x 4 that served as axles, some large nails, two wheels off a discarded tricycle, and two from an old baby carriage. A rusted nut and bolt held the front axle to the 2 x 8 body and a rope had been nailed at each end of the front to pull and steer the cart. But George, the old blacksmith, had made a few adjustments. He replaced the rope and attached a broken scoop shovel handle to the front 2 x 4 with a hinge. This made the cart manageable when walking downhill with it in tow.

As crude as it was, it served its purpose well as he transported empty soft drink bottles. Jimmy collected bottles where he could – from neighbors and from along roadsides where the more affluent tossed them after the contents had been drained. Each undamaged bottle was worth a two-cent refund at Mitchell's grocery store on Center Street. Jimmy ran his hand down the pocket of his overalls and fingered – for what seemed to be the one-hundredth time – his forty-six cents.

"Forty-six cents! I'll never get that bike at this rate."

He had been full of anticipation as he dragged the cartload of thirty bottles to Mitchell's earlier that afternoon. Thirty bottles! That was a good day's work. He had gathered all bottles his neighbors were willing to give up. Some neighbors saved bottles for their own children, but most kept them for Jimmy. So, thirty bottles was a good haul. But Mr. Mitchell found cracks or chips in seven of his bottles and the sixty cents he expected had suddenly been reduced to a mere forty-six cents.

🎁 🎁 🎁 🎁 🎁

Jimmy had turned seven in March of 1947 and the occasion had been anything but happy for Jimmy, his mother, and

57

sister. Jimmy's father had been badly wounded in the Normandy invasion. After a stay of some eight months in a hospital in England, he had been shipped home and discharged from the Army. He was home, but his health was frail. In January of that year he had come down with pneumonia. At the time he was working for a company that was building a new bridge on the highway that led into their middle Alabama town. Just six weeks later, he died. Jimmy's mother was left alone to fend for her nine-year-old daughter and her nearly seven-year-old son.

The family lived in a small frame house about a half-mile beyond the end of the pavement on Maple Street. After his father's death, his mother found work as a clerk at Davis' Drug Store. It barely paid for necessities. Any extras came from the little bit of money Jimmy earned collecting Coke bottles or running errands for some of their older neighbors. Although he was limited by his youth and small stature, he did the best he could. He could carry and stack firewood, but wielding an ax to split stove wood was still a little beyond his ability.

One day Mr. Mitchell said he might let Jimmy have an after-school job delivering groceries. However, he would have to have his own bicycle.

"I am not going to trust my paying customer's groceries to that rickety homemade cart," Mr. Mitchell told him.

"If I only had a bicycle," Jimmy thought again as he fingered the coins in his pocket.

He had managed to save ten dollars from odd jobs he performed during the summer. Mr. Wilburn now held those ten dollars as a deposit for the bicycle Jimmy wanted. Mr. Wilburn promised to hold the bike for Jimmy until the week before Christmas. If Jimmy could come up with the remaining money before then, the bicycle would be is. Otherwise, Mr. Wilburn would sell that bike to the first person who could pay the full price, and refund Jimmy his down-payment. Jimmy had managed to make two more payments to Mr. Wilburn, but he still owed eight dollars and twenty-eight cents. Counting the forty-six cents in his pocket, he had managed to save a grand total of two dollars and thirty-three cents. Now there was less than a week to go before Mr. Wilburn would let the bike go to the first person with the money. To make matters worse, three days ago when he had peeked through the frosted window at Wilburn's Western Auto, he had seen a man examining the bike and talking to Mr. Wilburn.

Jimmy let out a long, dejected sigh as he recalled the man talking to Mr. Wilburn.

"It will take a miracle to get that bike now," he said to himself as he puffed up the low hill that was Maple Street. The wheels on his rickety cart wobbled on the nails that held them to their 2 x 4 axles. The cart bounced and chattered as he pulled it over the gravel and rocks of the unpaved street.

"I wonder if there really are any such things as miracles?" he wondered as he turned off the dirt street and started up the lane that led to their house.

"I need some more stove wood, Jimmy," his sister, Nancy, called to him as he came through the back door into the kitchen from the porch. With their mother at work until after six every day but Sunday, nine-year-old Nancy became responsible for the household chores such as cleaning and cooking. These were really not jobs she disliked, at least most of the time. She enjoyed cooking and became quite good at it. The light cleaning chores of sweeping, bed making, and dusting, were okay, too. Everyone pitched in when washing dishes after the evening meal. Their mother made it a fun time of visiting and catching each other up on the day's events.

Jimmy's mother managed to find time for the heavier household chores like laundry. In warm weather, this job was done with a washboard and tub on the back porch. The chore was moved into the kitchen, though, when the weather turned damp and chilly, as it was now.

"Do you think there are really such things as miracles?" Jimmy asked his older sister as he reappeared through the kitchen door with an armload of stove wood for the wood box.

"Oh, I don't know," she said as she stirred the fire and poked another piece of wood into the coals.

"I prayed that God would send a miracle when Daddy was sick. I asked God to make him better, but he died anyway. Still, I don't know. Maybe there are miracles sometimes. After all, if they happened all the time, we wouldn't think of them as miracles. We would just come to expect that that is the way things are supposed to be."

"Pastor Mike said that God did make Daddy better in heaven," Jimmy said confidently.

"Yes, he did," Nancy agreed. "I guess heaven is a miracle, just like getting born on earth is a miracle when you really think about it. So, yes, Jimmy, I think I do believe that there really are such things as miracles, but you have to believe in them and then look at things really closely to see them for what they are. I guess if a person does that, they may catch a glimpse of heaven where other people would not see much of anything at all."

"I hope there really are such things as miracles. I could sure use one," Jimmy said as he turned to go after another armload of stove wood.

🎁 🎁 🎁 🎁 🎁

The week before Christmas 1947 came and went and Jimmy's miracle had not come. Despite his best efforts, three dollars and twelve cents was the best he could collect. Even worse, when he had gone by Wilburn's store to pay his money, the bike was gone. In fact, all the bikes were gone – sold out. When Jimmy asked to see Mr. Wilburn, the clerk told him that

Mr. Wilburn had gone to Selma to see about his mother who had fallen and broken her hip. He would probably be out of town until Christmas Eve. When Jimmy asked who bought the bike, the clerk said that Mr. Wilburn had sold it to a man at the Methodist Church.

Jimmy stood on the sidewalk in front of the Western Auto Store, his heart filled with disappointment. All summer and fall he had worked, saving every penny he could just to buy that bike. Now, it was less than one week before Christmas, and there was no bicycle, no refund, and only three dollars and twelve cents to do whatever Christmas shopping he might do for his mother and sister. As he moped along Main Street, he noticed a man in a Salvation Army uniform standing beside a kettle suspended on a tripod. The man was ringing a bell and greeted all who passed by with a hearty *"Merry Christmas."* Reaching into his pocket, Jimmy pulled out two nickels and two pennies. He held them tightly for a moment and then dropped them into the kettle.

"God bless you, son," the man said with an understanding smile.

"Why not?" Jimmy thought. The twelve cents would not do him that much good now. Besides, it made him feel better to think he might be helping someone even less well off than he was.

Further down Main Street, Jimmy passed the 5 & 10 where the smell of fresh popcorn lured him inside. This was as good a place as any to do his Christmas shopping. Moving slowly up and down the aisles and peering over the counters, he finally settled on a brightly colored floral apron for his sister. He then bought a pair of soft-looking slippers for his mother. With what was left from his three dollars, he splurged and bought a large bag of chocolate kisses. This was something all three of them could enjoy together.

On Christmas Eve he lay awake thinking about the Christmas Story that his mother had read to them from the Bible

61

before she tucked them into bed. He thought about the angels
and Baby Jesus. And he thought again about the frosted window
at Wilburn's Western Auto store. He thought about the times he
had peeked through that window and glimpsed the bike that he
hoped, by some miracle, would become his. As he lay in bed, he
whispered a prayer, "Dear Jesus, I wish I knew if there were
really such things as miracles."

On Christmas morning, he and Nancy sat around the
Christmas tree in the living room with their mother. They
admired the tree even though it was decorated only with simple
paper ornaments and strings of popcorn. They had opened and
admired their few gifts and had opened the bag of chocolate
kisses, each taking one. Just then there was a knock on the front
door. His mother rose to answer the knock. When the door
opened, Jimmy recognized the man on the other side as the same
man he had seen through the frosted window talking to Mr.
Wilburn about the bicycle.

"Ma'am," he asked, "do you have a seven-year-old boy
named Jimmy living here?"

"Why, yes. Yes, I do," answered his mother.

"Well, then I think I am at the right place," grinned the
man. "Santa was running late with his deliveries last night and
he asked me to help him out by bringing this here this morning."

With that, he rolled the shiny red and white bicycle into
the living room.

🎁 🎁 🎁 🎁 🎁

"Of course," Jim smiled as he opened his eyes and leaned
forward in his chair to approach his keyboard and begin writing
his sermon. How many times since that Christmas in 1947 had

he peered through the frosted window of faith and glimpsed a miracle?

"Of course, I know where that came from," he whispered to himself.

Just then the phone rang. It was Mary, Bob's wife.

"Thought you would like to know," she said, "the test results are back and it looks like the new chemo is working. Bob's blood work shows improvement and the tumor is shrinking. The doctor says he can probably go home for Christmas and next year is looking brighter!"

"Yes!" Jim said as he hung up the phone.

"Yes!" he repeated. "Mr. Wilburn's frosted window has come through again and I still believe in miracles."

He began typing the scripture for his sermon:

"Jesus answered and said unto them,
Go and show John again
those things which ye do hear and see:
The blind receive their sight,
and the lame walk,
the lepers are cleansed,
and the deaf hear,
the dead are raised up . . ."

Matthew 11:4-5

C. R. Hill, Jr.

About The Author

Dr. C. R. Hill, Jr., is an ordained United Methodist Minister in the North Georgia Conference of the United Methodist Church. He holds his AA degree from Emmanuel College in Franklin Springs, Georgia, his BSED degree from the University of Georgia in Athens, Georgia, and his MDIV and DMIN degrees from Emory University's Candler School of Theology in Atlanta, Georgia. Dr. Hill has served eleven congregations while under appointment in the pastoral ministry since 1963. He currently is serving as Senior Pastor of the Canton First United Methodist Church in the County Seat of Cherokee County, Georgia, one of the nation's fastest growing counties.

A U. S. Army Veteran, Dr. Hill served with the 2nd Armored Cavalry in Germany during the height of the Cold War. He began his ministry following his tour of duty in the military.

In addition to his pastoral assignments, Dr. Hill has served on numerous conference and district boards and agencies within the United Methodist Church, including the Board of Ordained Ministry for eight years, the Conference Committee on Global Ministries for eight years, and Chair of that Board for four years. He served as Chair of the Griffin District Committee on Ordained Ministries for eight years and was Dean of the North Georgia School of Christian Missions for two years. Currently, Dr. Hill serves on the Atlanta Marietta District Committee on

C. R. Hill, Jr.

Church Buildings and Locations as well as the Reinhardt College (Waleska, Georgia) Board of Trustees.

Dr. Hill has published two others book, *Between Two Worlds* and *Light Beyond the Veil*.

In November of 1962, Dr. Hill married his wife, Jackie, the former Jacqueline Daniel of Athens, Georgia. They have two married children and two grandsons.

Through The Frosted Window
Order Today!

Orders may be placed from the author:

Dr. C. R. Hill, Jr.
P. O. Box 4576
Canton, GA 30114-0216
www.thefrostedwindow.com
Make checks payable to *"The Frosted Window"*

OR from the publisher:

Patchwork Press, Ltd.
P. O. Box 4684
Canton, GA 30115
www.patchworkpress.com
Make checks payable to *"Patchwork Press, Ltd."*
Patchwork Press, Ltd. accepts Visa, MasterCard, and Discover
for your convenience.

Credit Card Number: _____

Name of Cardholder: _____

Expiration Date: _____

Through The Frosted Window

_____ copies @ $11.00 each = _____

Shipping and Handling Charges = _____

(Shipping and Handling Charges are $ 1.50 per book)

Ship to:

Name: _____

Address: _____

City, State, Zip: _____

Have you read other books from Patchwork Press, Ltd.?

Silver in the Slop (and other surprises!)
$ 12.00 (includes sales tax)
by Cathy Lee Phillips

Gutsy Little Flowers
$ 13.00 (includes sales tax)
by Cathy Lee Phillips

Silver Reflections: A Daily Journal
$ 17.00 (includes sales tax)
by Cathy Lee Phillips

Aging, Ailments, and Attitudes
$ 17.00 (includes sales tax)
by Cathy Lee Phillips

For further information, contact Patchwork Press, Ltd.
P. O. Box 4684
Canton, GA 30115
770-720-7988
www.patchworkpress.com

George E. Morris speaks about C. R. Hill, Jr. and Through The Frosted Window . . .

"This book is an outstanding example of the powerful significance and effectiveness of narrative theology and narrative preaching. All of us enjoy stories and have a profound appreciation for gifted story-tellers. Moreover, all of us are shaped by stories.

This is precisely why the Bible itself, when taken as a whole, is a vast "Story Book." Even those parts of the Bible that do not fit the traditional narrative form (e.g., epistles and proverbs), can only be adequately understood and interpreted in terms of the Bible's overall narrative framework.

Dr. Hill is one of our most gifted narrative preachers. The fact that he is a poet gives an added dimension to the power and effectiveness of his story-telling. He brings all of these gifts to bear upon the most significant story of all – THE CHRISTMAS STORY. He focuses on the beautiful story of Jesus' birth without falling into the trap of presenting a romantic view of the Christ child which suffers from a "disconnect" with the hard realities of our everyday life.

C. R. Hill, Jr., knows very well that at the birth of Jesus "all was *not* calm and bright!" He is careful, therefore, to connect HIS STORY, i.e., the Gospel Story, with our stories.

He does not treat the birth of Jesus as a romantic departure from the pain, confusion, loneliness, conflict and multiple needs of life as we experience it in this world. Rather, Dr. Hill's stories highlight how God has met our deepest needs in and through the Bethlehem Gift.

Laity and clergy alike will profit greatly from this remarkable little book."

--George E. Morris
Dan and Lillian Hankey Senior Professor of World Evangelism
The World Methodist Council